GII

The Language of
The Human Heart

Fr. Michael Briese

Copyright © 2019, Michael Briese

ISBN: 978-0-9980231-2-0

Library of Congress Control Number: 2019950583

Scripture texts in this work are taken from the New American Bible, revised edition © 2010, 1991, 1986, 1970 Confraternity of Christian Doctrine, Washington, D.C., and are used by permission of the copyright owner. All Rights Reserved. No part of the New American Bible may be reproduced in any form without permission in writing from the copyright owner.

Printed in the United States of America.

OTHER BOOKS BY FR. MICHAEL BRIESE

Gifts of God's Grace
More Gifts of God's Grace
God's Mercy
St. Paul: Disciple, Teacher, Servant of Christ
Longing for God's Presence
Love: What a Great Gift!
Journey of a Heart on Fire
As God Speaks: Reflections on Holy Scripture
Our Lord Among Us
Spiritual Common Sense
Forgiveness: Freedom by Letting Go
Living the Gospel: A Journey Through Discipleship
Living with a Disciple's Heart: Being Attuned to Our Lord
In Search of Solitude
The Beauty Within
Compassion: The Root of Justice
Teach Me Your Ways
Reflections of a Life Lived in Christ
Charismata

*Rich and Poor: Seeking the Common Good by
    Striving to Build Up the Kingdom of God*
A Life in Christ
Works of Mercy and Service

Dedicated to those whose frail, imperfect and broken human heart, mind or spirit thirst, even deeply desire, God's immense mercy, undeserved forgiveness and greater love.

*"Lord, teach me to be generous,
to serve you as you deserve,
to give and not to count the
cost, to fight and not to heed the
wounds, to toil and not to seek
for rest, to labor and not to ask
for reward, save that of knowing
that I am doing your will.*

Amen."

—St. Ignatius Loyola

"The only plans I have are the plans I have not made since I wait in expectation, listen with an attentive heart, and actively pursue my lifelong intention to go forth with God."

—Fr. Michael Briese

Table of Contents

Introduction xiii

Prayer: xiv

Gift of Prayer xv

*Preface: Prayer Is the Light of the Soul
by St. John Chrysostom* xvii

I   Conversations with God: 1

    1.   Our Father (with Meditation) 1
    2.   Reflections on the Our Father 2
    3.   Thank You, O Lord 4
    4.   O Lord, My God (A Desire for Closeness with God) 7
    5.   Hear, O Lord, and Answer Me 8
    6.   Healing 11
    7.   Suffering 13
    8.   Cries of the Heart 14
    9.   Gift of Life 15

Gift of Prayer

    10. Expectation 18

    11. If Only 21

    12. Teach Me, Lord (with Meditation) . . 25

    13. Teach Me Your Ways. 27

    14. Stillness (a Meditation) 39

    15. A Solitary Heart 48

    16. Dear Holy Spirit 50

II   **Prayers for Others:** **51**

    1. Prayer for the Army of Pray-ers . . . 51

    2. Prayer of Support for Students and Young Adults. 53

    3. Prayer for Veterans 54

    4. Prayer for Farmers 55

    5. Prayers for Priests. 57

    6. Prayer for Addicts by Reinhold Niebuhr. 58

III   **The Beatitudes:**. **59**

    1. Pope Francis's Modern Beatitudes . . 59

    2. The Beatitudes 60

Michael Briese

3.	The Beatitudes as Prayer 62
4.	Who Are My Neighbors (a Meditation) 64
5.	Golden Roses 69

IV Prayers for Holy Days: 71

1. Marian Prayers (2) 71
2. Prayer for the New Year 73
3. OH! Ancient Night 75
4. OH! Ancient Day 76
5. OH! Glorious Moment 78
6. A Prayer for Pentecost 80
7. Corpus Christi Sunday Prayer (Body of Christ) 82

V Blessings: 84

1. Prayer for Deacons 84
2. Prayer for Healing through Fr. Al Schwartz 85
3. Mother's Day Blessing 86
4. Father's Day Blessing 87

Gift of Prayer

5.	Blessing for Grandparents	88
6.	Blessing for Those Who Have Disabilities	89
7.	Queenship of the Blessed Virgin Mary	92
8.	Final Blessing	94
9.	A Prayer	95
10.	Prayer I	96
11.	Prayer II	105
12.	Prayer III	115

INTRODUCTION

This brief work is but a collection of prayers I composed over many years under various circumstances. They include poetic prayers, written works reflecting heartfelt cries, different styles and ways to pray. There are many ways to pray. Also included here are a small number of prayers written, or at least credited, to other great people of God. I hope this work will help you as you seek to learn more about prayer, and HOW to pray and WHY we pray. Peace and blessings unto you as you journey along on your lifelong heartfelt quest to draw closer to our dear Lord and to find peace and rest in the company of Christ.

Dear God,

"...we lift up all priests:

May they, through the modesty and humility of their lives, commit themselves actively to a solidarity with those who are the most poor."

Pope Francis
June, 2019

GIFT OF PRAYER

Given the Gift of Prayer,

I now pray with all my heart.

Taught to trust,

I now trust others.

Given the freedom to question,

I wonder thoughts and ask others.

Shown the sacredness in work,

I now realize the grace present in daily labor.

With the gift of understanding,

I strive to be more understanding.

Love given freely by strangers

Gift of Prayer

encourages me to be a Good Samaritan.

Weary of human suffering,

I see prejudice, hunger and war and pray for Peace.

Keenly aware of my human limitations,

I strive to appreciate the gifts of being human.

Aware of the bountiful gifts of the human heart,

I see why every person is a Treasure

in both Image and Likeness.

Michael Briese

PRAYER IS THE LIGHT OF THE SOUL

by St. John Chrysostom

The highest good is prayer and conversation with God because it means that we are in God's company and in union with Him. When light enters our human or physical eyes, our eyesight is sharpened; when a soul is intent on God, God's inextinguishable light shines into it and makes it bright and clear. I am talking, of course, of prayer that comes from the heart and not from routine: not the prayer that is assigned to particular days or particular moments in time, but the prayer that happens continuously by day and by night.

Indeed, the soul should not turn to God only at times of specific prayer. Whatever we are engaged in, whether it is care for the poor, some other duty or some act of generosity, we

Gift of Prayer

should remember God and long for God. The love of God will be as salt is to food, making our actions into a perfect dish to set before the Lord of all things. Then it is right that we should receive the fruits of our labors, overflowing onto us through all eternity if we have been offering them to Him throughout our lives.

Prayer is the light of the soul, true knowledge of God and a mediator between God and men. Prayer lifts the soul into the heavens where it hugs God in an indescribable embrace. The soul seeks the milk of God like a baby crying for the breast. It fulfills its own vows and receives in exchange gifts better than anything that can be seen or imagined.

Prayer is a go-between linking us to God. It gives joy to the soul and calms its emotions. I warn you though, do not imagine that prayer is simply words. Prayer is the desire for God, an indescribable devotion not given by man but brought about by God's grace. As St. Paul says: *For when we cannot choose words in order to pray properly, the Spirit himself intercedes on our behalf in a way that could never be put into words.*

Michael Briese

If God gives someone the gift of such prayer, it is a gift of imperishable riches, a heavenly food that satisfies the spirit. Whoever tastes that food catches fire and his soul burns forever with desire for the Lord.

To begin on this path, start by adorning your house with modesty and humility. Make it shine brightly with the light of justice. Decorate it with the gold leaf of good works and with the jewels of faithfulness and greatness of heart. Finally, to make the house perfect, raise a gable above it all, a gable of prayer. Thus, you will have prepared a pure and sparkling house for the Lord. Receive the Lord into this royal and splendid dwelling, in other words, receive, by His grace, His image into the temple of your soul.

OUR FATHER

Our Father who art in heaven . . .

Hallowed be thy name . . .

Thy kingdom come . . .

Thy will be done, on earth as it is in heaven . . .

Give us this day our daily bread . . .

Forgive us our trespasses, as we forgive those who trespass against us . . .

Lead us not into temptation . . .

But deliver us from evil.

—**Fr. Pedro Arupe, SJ**

REFLECTIONS ON THE OUR FATHER

The Gospels remind us about the "Our Father" taught to us by Jesus. We gather at church as people of faith. With prayerful eyes and ears, we turn to our Lord and we ask that we may be blessed in faith and prayer. We pray that we may be able to discern God's will, that our desire to more fully grasp and know God will be granted, and that we may be granted the gifts with which we can grow in virtue, prayer and holiness.

God our Father gives us faith to enlighten our minds, to open our hearts and to renew our lives. In prayer, we ask our Lord to journey in our company all the days of our lives. We ask our Father to give light where once there was only darkness, direction where once there was only distraction, and trust where once there was only doubt. We ask our Father to come into the

Michael Briese

very depths of all whose hearts cry out. Our Father hears the cries of the poor, the sick, the lost and those who are paralyzed in disbelief. Amid the darkness of the human heart, we can, in fact, discover and come to rest in the presence of God. He is at once present to us and yet, by His nature, God is beyond the human realm. Our Father grants us a prayerful spirit, and as such, we often can see more clearly, even amid the blindness or darkness of our own heart. Through prayer we can see, hear, listen, more clearly understand and discern our Father's will. Let us give thanks to the Lord our God.

THANK YOU, O LORD

Thank You, O Lord, for letting me live another day.

Thank You, O Lord, for the provision of adequate shelter.

Thank You, O Lord, for the many gifts of adequate food, crops, waterways and other beneficial natural resources.

Thank You, O Lord, for the bountiful crops of the fields, fruits of the orchards and various livestock.

Thank You, O Lord, for the abundant beauties we can discover or find in and around us and all throughout creation.

Michael Briese

Thank You, O Lord, for our loving parents and their exemplary justice, kindness, mercy and forgiveness.

Thank You, O Lord, for Your infinite love, merciful justice and deep concern for us, our loved ones, our neighbors and even the strangers in need.

Thank You, O Lord, for this morning and the radiant, fiery orange rays which permeate the breaking of dawn, as the late night surrenders unto the breaking new day.

Thank You, O Lord, for this breath You just granted me.

Thank You, O Lord, as each passing second and moment sustains Your love for all human life.

Thank You, O Lord, for creating me out of Your infinite love and creating me in Your image and likeness.

Thank You, O Lord, for granting me this one gift of one lifetime and enabling me to more fully understand that all human life is sacred, precious and holy.

Thank You, O Lord, for granting to me, an unworthy servant, Your unearned, unmerited and undeserved divine mercy. Holy are You, O Lord, our God.

Thank You, O Lord, for all You say and do in, and throughout each and every hour of my lifetime. I search and discover You in my midst. I wait, and I wait, as You, dear Lord, enter more fully into the very depths of my heart, mind and soul. Blessed are You, dear Lord.

In thanksgiving, say one Our Father and reflect upon the words.

O LORD, MY GOD

O Lord, my God, I have the heartfelt desire to enter more fully into Your company. I seek to follow in the footsteps of Your beloved Son, our Savior Jesus Christ. My heart wrestles with Your angels, yet I strive to remain attentive to You, dear Lord, and to the ancient wisdom of the Holy Spirit. Throughout the hours of each passing day, I strive to live my life in accordance with Your will. Still, I fall short, even fail, all too often. Yet, I persist! Your test of any human being is but a mere taste of Your infinite divine mercy. Holy are You, dear Lord. I am humbled by Your immense mercy, justice and compassion. At times when evening has arrived and night is about to settle in, I am able and willing to humbly discover and receive Your unconditional gift of blessed spiritual renewal. Holy are You, O Lord, my God.

HEAR, O LORD, AND ANSWER ME...

Come to me, O Lord, my God, come to me. Be with me. Stand beside me. Walk with me, O Lord, my God. You are my only Hope. Your tender love, Your grace and the silence of Your gentle presence guide me through each day. You alone are the Joy of my daily life. You alone guide me at my side. You give me the courage to live, knowing that one day we shall be together. You are the foundation of my heartfelt thoughts and prayers. I trust in You.

You give me strength each day. You provide counsel in the silent echoes of the warm, heartfelt words of ancient days and nights. You touch my soul. You strengthen me. Your graceful love stirs my need to set aside time for You. Who am I if I cannot make time for the very One whose unconditional love created me and gave me the precious gift of life? O Lord, in

Michael Briese

Your own image and likeness, You gave me my first breath. You gave me the gift of Love—a gift to be passed on to others.

Why, O Lord, have You, in Your Almighty Wisdom, given me this living treasure of human life? You chose me to share your love with others, for it is in giving that one shall receive. Still, O Lord, how am I to know You, to love You and to serve You with all my heart? O Lord, I have come to You thankful for Your steadfast love. O Lord, You alone stand beside me each day as I live out the daily gifts You give unto me.

Slowly over time, You have molded my frail human heart. You have transformed my human spirit, changed my daily quest, provided guidance as needed, and shown me the gift of patience, which all too often can be a tiresome burden. Still, patience makes listening easier, prayer less cumbersome, and understanding more generous. It truly calls forth one's willingness to give of one's self unto others and to transform the human spirit through that kind and patient giving of one's self.

Gift of Prayer

This is most visible when one gives gently, quietly and patiently. Heartfelt love is not hidden; rather, it radiates the Spirit of the Lord! It is quiet but steadfast, patient but persistent, gentle but strong. This is God's Love to be discovered in the human heart.

HEALING

Lord, O Lord, we cry out to You for You are indeed our God, and we, Your people. Lord, make haste to help. Illness and despair have struck at my beloved one. Indeed, she is living a life initially created and formed by You in Your image and likeness. Human in nature, she is worthy and deserves Your infinite and undivided divine love, divine mercy and divine healing. You, O Lord, can make haste to help us care for her. Hear the prayers crying out for Your divine and miraculous works. You, O Lord, can bring healing to those who suffer illness, despair or spiritual emptiness. Lord, please hear these cries. We beseech You, all the angels of heaven and all those whose hearts aspire to turn to You. Hear, O Lord, the cries of all seeking Your divine healing, renewal and recovery. We ask You, dear Lord, to answer our prayers for healing, for greater graces, for our human brokenness, and for the perseverance needed to confront and manage any suffering. Lord, grant

Gift of Prayer

us a deeper sense of understanding, acceptance, gratitude and awe on our part toward You and Your infinite love, mercy and justice. We give honor and glory to You, our God. Truly, Your name is the one and true Holy Name. Amen.

SUFFERING

Lord, human life initiated by Your divine love cries out in suffering. Lord, though voices might be stilled, our hearts are indeed restless and groping for greater clarity and understanding. Dear Lord, You hear the cries of the human heart. O God, we beg You to step forth, enter more fully into the company of Your people and bring healing to Your children. Come, dear Lord, hear our cries as they echo throughout Your heavens. Hear, O Lord, as we wait for You to answer us. Amen.

CRIES OF THE HEART

Lord, my God, where are You? We cry out and beseech You now, at this VERY moment. Hear us, dear Lord! Hear the cries of many troubled hearts! What are we to say in words? What are we to do? Speak, O Lord. We wait in silence and solitude. Speak, dearly beloved Creator. Draw near to all who suffer. Come closer and rest in our company. Make haste, dear Lord. We wait and will continue to wait. Lord, bring healing, greater courage and divine mercy. Many hearts await You, dear Lord. Send forth Your Spirit and bring healing, renewal and resolve. Hear our prayers, dear Lord. For now, we wait in expectation. Indeed, You are our God, and we are Your beloved children. Hear, O Lord, and answer us. Amen.

GIFT OF LIFE

O Lord, life is Your most awesome gift! Precious, sacred, holy, invaluable, a treasure to behold! In Your own image and likeness, You breathe new life. You created man and woman, and they gave the promise of life to each generation. O Lord, my God, You bless the gift of life with bountiful creation. You give us the sun and moon and stars, the lands and waterways, the animals of the forests and the fish of the seas. We are fruitful. Bountiful are each and every generation. O Lord, You stooped down and walked among us to breathe eternal glory and to bring redemption to human life.

O Lord, there is none beside You. You are our God . . . our God of time before humanity, our God of ancient days and our God who is and always shall be. You are as You have always been and shall be throughout eternity. Glorious God, Lover of life, Creator of all that has been and ever shall be, You are the vibrant source of human renewal and regeneration.

O Lord, You are present amid the lilies of the field, the cattle on the plains, the fish of the waterways and every man, woman and child. Lord, walk with us. Lord, You walk amid the morning dew, the half-day moment of noon, amid the twilight of the passing day, and even amid the darkness of the late-night hours. O Lord, You are my God! You are the source of every breath I take, every moment I live and every ounce of love.

God, in Your infinite wisdom, You took clay and molded every ounce of bone and sinew into man, woman and child. In Your divine humility, You chose to create out of pure divine love. You chose life! O God, You are our divine source of life. We come before You in awe, humility and thanksgiving. O Lord, You are the joy of human life!

O Lord, walk with me. You are indeed holy! O Lord, You created life and the love needed to bring forth new life and countless generations. Indeed, You are precious! Lord, all holiness flows from You. The gift of life has brought endless ages. O Lord, only with You will humanity come to see that glorious moment when God and humanity will enjoy the fullness of eternal union.

O Lord, Creator of all that has been, is now, and ever shall be, we come before You this day, this very moment, to give thanks for Your immense love and the gift of life. O Lord, there is none beside You! You are our God, this day, tomorrow and always. Lord, bless You for creation. Bless You for life. O Lord, bless You, for You are our God, holy indeed and the fountain of all holiness. You are the source of all life. You are the source of true love! O God, Your very being is infinite love! Precious is the gift of life!

EXPECTATION

The only plans I have are the plans I have not made since I wait in expectation, listen with an attentive heart, and actively pursue my lifelong intention to go forth with God. Lord, You journey in my company. My days are numbered. You bless me with life, the breaking of every dawn, time itself, every breath I take, the countless beauties discovered throughout creation and, most important, Your provision of Your Spirit which rests within me.

O God, my God, You walk in my company and are always willing to provide the Light of the World in the midst of my human brokenness. Lord, Your tender words, infinite love and immense compassion bring healing, change and renewal to my human imperfection.

O Lord, I ask, "Who am I to make plans for my life as I live each day with a sweet awareness of Your eternal presence? Each hour of each day is Your time, dear Lord. Who am I to fully grasp and understand Your very presence? Who am I to determine just WHAT You have in store for me this very day?"

Lord, I abandon my own wants and plans and instead, I wait . . . I wait for You, O Lord . . . to gather and find rest and stillness within the very depth of my heart and to make clear what You ask of me this hour, this day. And so, I wait . . . Come, dear Lord . . . gather within the very depths of my heart. Lord, make clear what You ask of me this very day.

O God, my God, You sent Your only beloved Son to invite Your people to draw near. Your Holy Spirit echoes this ancient divine invitation within the very depths of countless broken lives. Lord, slow us down. Teach us to read Holy Scripture, to pray and nourish the wisdom of our heart, to seek Your justice and good counsel and to listen carefully to others. O Lord, teach me Your ways, encourage me to persevere as I learn about our faith, and HOW to live out Your Holy Gospel as I strive to put my faith into action.

Gift of Prayer

Lord, I pray, and humanity prays, that You will grant all peoples and nations Your peace. You make time to walk in my company, and for this lifelong blessing of divine mercy, I give thanks to You, my dear Lord. Blessed are You, O Lord, our God. Holy is Your name.

O Lord, I wait in expectation and am keenly aware that my life is truly Your life. O Lord, in the end, there are three great gifts . . . Faith, Hope and Love . . . and the greatest of these is Love. Lord, take my one life and make me a true and greater gift of Your love. My dear Lord, I offer You this prayer in a spirit of awe, humility and thanksgiving.

IF ONLY ...

If only I could be closer to You, dear Lord. If I could just reach out my hand and touch You and feel Your infinite and merciful touch. If only I could grasp You in a mere moment of my full understanding of You, my beloved Lord and God. Where are You at the moments when I strive to see You, to more fully know You and to evermore completely love You? I do not know where You are. Still, even amid the darkness of the late night, I watch for You. I know not when You will arrive here at my side. I dream dreams of moments when I felt lonely, isolated, ignored, even unknown. It was then You seemed so far away. However, there in such moments—moments of darkness, moments when despair seemed to prevail, it was then that I persevered and believed.

In such times I came to discover that the Light of the World will always prevail. I prayed and asked You to come closer, to draw near, and You responded to my soft prayerful cries, "If only I could be in Your presence." In such moments, my heart would awaken, my mind became more attentive, and my spirit was blessed with immense love, simplicity and greater trust. Amid the breaking of that spiritual dawn, I was blessed by You, dear Lord. You had entered into the darkness of my spirit, picked me up, and rested me in the very depths of Your one holy and blessed Sacred Heart. Those moments were sacred, precious and holy moments.

Lord, my God, if only I could be where You are at all moments. I truly desire to know You, to praise You and to love You with all my heart, all my mind and all my spirit. I bear this one broken, imperfect and impaired prayerful desire; yet, I wait. I wait patiently, O Lord. I trust You are in my company; Yet, I know not where, or how or through whom. So, I must wait. And wait, I have done.

I know not that hour when You, dear Lord, will enter more fully into my heart of hearts. There amid the silence of my heart, You, dear Lord enter into my broken heart. There Lord, You lift me up, take my hand and carry me through the darkness of night. It is in such moments that I discover Your infinite Sacred Heart—a Divine Heart blessed with love, healing, renewal, and greater faith, greater hope and greater love. During the breaking of each dawn, I trust and I believe that my heartfelt desire to rest in Your company will always prevail over my brokenness, despair or cries. You, dear Lord, light the way as I journey along the long and winding road of life.

Lord, I beg You to enter more fully into countless lives. Send forth Your beloved and steadfast modern disciples. Guide them to reach out to and serve our fellow frail and imperfect human beings. We are all brothers and sisters, yet, so many of us, dear Lord, stand divided. Our hearts are restless, our minds wander aimlessly and our human spirit appears to be chained to the foolish ways of this world. My dearly beloved Lord, we pray You will continue to send forth Your infinite love, good counsel and divine mercy. We plead for You to bless countless impaired lives and nourish them with Your infinite love and heartfelt wisdom.

Gift of Prayer

Lord, into Your presence, I entrust my deep, heartfelt pleas. As I find rest in Your divine company, I ask You, dear Lord, to hear my prayers and to grant them in accordance with Your own will. I ask all this in the Holy Name of Jesus Christ, whose Sacred Heart invites all Your peoples to draw near and find stillness, rest and divine company. For this I give my deep, heartfelt thanks to You, my dearly beloved Lord. Amen.

TEACH ME, LORD

Teach me, Lord,
to continue in prayers
of adoration to You.

Know, Lord,
that my heart cries out
to You for Your guidance.

Please, Lord!
Help me to overcome distractions.

Please, Lord!
Fill me with Your life-giving
Spirit of Love.

Please, Lord!
Grant me the trust I need
to grow in my love for You.

Please, Lord,
Source of all Hope,
guide me to serve you.

Gift of Prayer

Please, Lord,
Teacher of prayer,
please give me a charitable heart.

Lord, know that I seek
Your forgiveness of my sins
and reconciliation of my heart.

Understand, O Lord,
I come to You
with a spirit of thanksgiving.

TEACH ME YOUR WAYS

Lord, teach me to follow in your footsteps, to bring Your love into the lives of others, to feed the hungry, clothe the naked, visit the sick and the dying, care for the widow and orphan, help the stranger in need and serve the least among us. Lord, enable me to uphold the dignity of all people, including those who are weak, vulnerable and without a strong voice . . . most notably, the unborn and persons with disabilities. Lord, teach me to learn from the little ones. Teach me to see You through the lives of the poor in spirit and those whose lives are afflicted by addiction. Lord, bless me with the ability to hear Your heartfelt wisdom in the words of my elders, the ill and the suffering. Hear me, O Lord! Grant me the courage, perseverance and humility needed to imitate You. Lord, teach me to recognize You wherever I go. O Lord, guide me and bless me in ways everlasting. Lord, I ask You to grant this prayer. In peace I humbly give thanks to You, my Lord and my God. Amen.

Prayer is the road on which you are chosen to walk humbly in search of our Lord. Live out your faith by putting your faith into action. Be not afraid to journey in the company of Christ. This is the Lord's Day, and your own life is one of the great treasures our Lord creates. Live out your holiness by putting your faith into action. Listen, as John writes, "Beloved, we are God's children now; what we shall be has not yet been revealed. We do know that when it is revealed, we shall be like him, for we shall see him as he is. Everyone who has this hope based on him makes himself pure, as he is pure" (1 Jn 3:2–3). In your ongoing relationship with our Lord and Savior Jesus Christ, remember that "When Christ your life appears, then you too will appear with him in glory. Put to death, then, the parts of you that are earthly: immorality, impurity, passion, evil desire, and the greed that is idolatry" (Col 3:4–5).

Hear our good and gracious Lord and answer His divine invitation to draw near, to walk humbly in His company and to continue this life in His presence. Be not afraid to enter into a lifelong journey in the company of Christ. St. Paul writes, "The Spirit itself bears witness with our spirit that we are children of God, and if children, then heirs, heirs of God and joint heirs with Christ, if only we suffer with him so that we may also be glorified with him" (Rom 8:16-17). "For those who are led by the Spirit of God are children of God" (Rom 8:14). What matters is more than theology and philosophy; it is about the way we freely choose to live our lives. Put your faith into action.

Ask the Lord to take you by your hand and to lead you through the countless challenges involved in daily life. Be a child of God who looks around and sees God's many gifts and realizes that God does indeed call you forth. St. John writes, "This is how all will know that you are my disciples, if you have love for one another" (Jn 13:35). Be humbled and gracious that our great Lord speaks to you, through you and in you. Your holiness shines forth. Certainly, you have your own foibles and imperfections. Recognize and acknowledge this realization; however, you also possess a holy nature and

Gift of Prayer

the workings of the Holy Spirit. Accept God's invitation to you, hear His divine words, and be humbled by His divine invitation. Jesus said, "By this is my Father glorified, that you bear much fruit and become my disciples" (Jn 15:8). As you journey through this God-given gift of life, know that, "The honesty of the upright guides them; the faithless are ruined by their duplicity" (Prv 11:3). Live this holy life as you journey each hour and each day of your life upon the stairway to heaven. Be your kind and gentle self. Know that "By the sin of their lips the wicked are ensnared, but the just escape from a tight spot. . . . Whoever speaks honestly testifies truly, but the deceitful make lying witnesses" (Prv 12:13, 17). Listen as our Lord whispers within the silence of your heart.

Always seek to live out God's ways and not only your own ways. Be humbled as you get older. Acknowledge how little knowledge you really possess. In the scheme of human history, your little mind bears little knowledge. Be humbled and a person of thanksgiving; otherwise, pride, conceit and self-centeredness can step in and make it almost impossible for you to practice and live out a virtuous life. Recognize your own insignificance in human history, then give thanks to God for His many, many blessings. St. John wrote, "And now, children, remain in him, so that when he appears we may have confidence and not be put to shame by him at his coming" (1 Jn 2:28). Always choose to go with God! Then freely, willingly and knowingly, walk humbly in the company of our good Lord and Savior Jesus Christ! Last but not least, stand there, right now, at this moment, stand in awe and give thanks to God. Indeed, our Lord is with you!

Wherever this life journey takes you, whether it be all around the world, or living on a farm in the country or throughout the many cities which dot our society, always be prepared to listen to our Lord. Seek wisdom over pleasure. Seek to grow in your capacity to love. Hate no one. Forgive those who trespass against you. Be merciful and just. Do no harm either to yourself or others. Know that our Lord is with you through this one God-given lifetime. Remember, as Christ said, "Do not let your hearts be troubled. You have faith in God; have faith also in me. In my Father's house there are many dwelling places. If there were not, would I have told you that I am going to prepare a place for you? And if I go and prepare a place for you, I will come back again and take you to myself, so that where I am you also may be" (Jn 14:1–3). Take this daily journey, keenly aware of our Lord's infinite and immense love for you, then, give glory and praise to our God!

Allow our dear Creator to change and transform you into a quiet but strong soldier of God. Be shaped in God's ways and not merely your own ways. And if you say or believe that God cannot do this, simply stand back, and realize and acknowledge that God can do anything. St. Paul persecuted Christians. St. Peter denied Christ. St. Thomas doubted our Lord. Men and women can become the people our Lord invites them to become. Hopefully, you are blessed with a long life. Give this day and every day to our Lord. Understand that, with all your brokenness, God's many graces and gifts can indeed transform you into the person our Lord wants you to be. Realize the following: "All of us, gazing with unveiled face on the glory of the Lord, are being transformed into the same image from glory to glory, as from the Lord who is the Spirit" (2 Cor 3:18). Also realize, "If we live in the Spirit, let us also follow the Spirit. Let us not be conceited, provoking one another, envious of one another" (Gal 5:25-26). Change awaits your heartfelt desire to walk humbly in the company of Christ. Listen!

Flee into the very depths of your being. Find stillness and quiet, and pray. Listen and listen more! Allow your heart to open up and be attentive to the ways of Jesus Christ and the wisdom of the Holy Spirit. Hark back to ancient days when a psalmist, in deep prayer, wrote the following words: "That I may praise God's name in song and glorify it with thanksgiving. That will please the LORD more than oxen, more than bulls with horns and hooves" (Ps 69:31-32). Your heart, mind and soul are worth far more than oxen or bulls. Trust in our Lord. Allow our Lord to manifest in you the basics—faith, hope, love, mercy, kindness, compassion, justice, knowledge, understanding and wisdom. It is written, "Those who offer praise as a sacrifice honor me; I will let him whose way is steadfast look upon the salvation of God" (Ps 50:23). Go where God takes you and sing in a spirit of thanksgiving and give glory, honor and praise to the Divine Artist who creates you and molds you into the new person you are called to be.

Victory in Christ is yours for the asking. Our Lord invites you to come closer, to draw near and to pray. In prayer, seek all the Lord has to grant you. Seek the Lord! Search for Truth! Ask the Spirit of God to descend upon you and to grant you countless blessings. Be a person whose faith is paramount, whose daily life reflects that of Christ and whose words contain faith, hope and love. Understand the following: "But thanks be to God, who always leads us in triumph in Christ and manifests through us the odor of the knowledge of him in every place" (2 Cor 2:14). Victory is yours for the asking.

Each and every day, whisper these ancient words written by a psalmist, "In my heart I treasure your promise, that I may not sin against you" (Ps 119:11). Our Lord bestows upon you this one lifetime, many days and countless breaths. Give glory and honor to God. Look not that far and realize the many signs of God that appear each day throughout creation. At once, be humbled and impressed by God. He speaks to us throughout each passing hour and every passing day. This hour God grants you, but do you not realize that you really do not know for certain that you will have tomorrow? What an astonishing realization and a humbling understanding. God does hear you and speaks to you. Listen! Our Lord assured us when He said, "My sheep hear my voice; I know them, and they follow me. I give them eternal life, and they shall never perish. No one can take them out of my hand. My Father, who has given them to me, is greater than all, and no one can take them out of the Father's hand" (Jn 10:27-29). Stand in the company of Christ and go with God.

Love the Lord with all your heart, mind and soul. Understand you have a place, a role and a purpose in building up the modern Church. You are a member, a part and possess a purpose in the unfolding of God's Kingdom here at hand. Listen to our Lord! Listen! Understand this, "I give you a new commandment: love one another. As I have loved you, so you also should love one another. This is how all will know that you are my disciples, if you have love for one another" (Jn 13:34-35). Love and love even those you might not like. Love because it's what Christ did. Love because it is the greatest power you possess as a human being. As that Day approaches, be attentive to the loving Spirit who blesses you time and again. Stand in awe and be a truly thankful child of God.

When God the Father sent forth His only begotten Son, Jesus Christ, He sent forth this ancient message, "In him we have redemption by his blood, the forgiveness of transgressions, in accord with the riches of his grace" (Eph 1:7). Pay close attention as God speaks to you! Give ear to our Lord! Read Holy Scripture understanding the following, "Lovers of your law have much peace; for them there is no stumbling block" (Ps 119:165). Also read these ancient words, "The revelation of your words sheds light, gives understanding to the simple" (Ps 119:130). Allow our Lord to quietly enter into your daily life, take you by your hand and guide you on that ancient road to the everlasting life. Then, give thanks to God.

Lord, You are my holy Teacher! You take my hands and fold them together, and, standing, sitting or kneeling, I grasp my folded hands, and in a spirit of prayerful humility, I ask You for good counsel, divine mercy and forgiveness.

It is written, "Cast your care upon the Lord, who will give you support. He will never allow the righteous to stumble" (Ps 55:23). Give your whole self, the very depths of your being, and your heart, mind and soul over to our Lord. In return, you shall reap and enjoy God's divine care and mercy. "Many are the troubles of the righteous, but the Lord delivers him from them all" (Ps 34:20). "As they prayed, the place where they were gathered shook, and they were all filled with the holy Spirit and continued to speak the word of God with boldness" (Acts 4:31). Pray and pray more. Be awed by God's immense love, mercy and justice.

Do not fall prey to temptation. Let not temptation be the victor over you. When temptation hits you, immediately fall to your knees, or seek silence and pray, or call down the ample graces of the Holy Spirit. Use your capacity to pray as a major defense against sin and temptation. Understand that, at all times, our Lord is with you. The question to ask is, "Are you always with our Lord?" Be assured as it is written, "No trial has come to you but what is human. God is faithful and will not let you be tried beyond your strength; but with the trial he

Gift of Prayer

will also provide a way out, so that you may be able to bear it" (1 Cor 10:13).

In the end, draw closer to our Lord. It is written, "You belong to God, children, and you have conquered them, for the one who is in you is greater than the one who is in the world" (1 Jn 4:4). The world is filled with empty promises, broken dreams and even nightmares and misery. Be not afraid to go out into this world carrying within you the Light of Christ with flames brightly shining. You are indeed holy, sacred and precious. Go forth into the world and bring the love of God, the mercy of Christ and the wisdom of the Holy Spirit to those whose lives you cross. Allow our God to guide you in ways everlasting. Be or become a person of thanksgiving. Be a modern disciple of Jesus Christ. "And over all these put on love, that is, the bond of perfection" (Col 3:14). In the end, give glory and praise to God! Then, go off and find stillness, silence and pray.

STILLNESS

O Lord, my God, it is in the stillness of the human heart that I discover You. I must go off to that corner of my world where, there within the silence, You speak. O Lord, You speak to the faithful reminding us about the ancient covenant we share with You. You call us to walk amid the barren days and to renew Your presence in the lives of others. If only we would make the time to listen as You, O Lord, whisper in the stillness of the heart. Lord, let no man, woman or child journey through this life without first realizing that the face of God is at hand! You, O Lord, stand here in our presence. If only we would seek You in the silence of the human heart. There, in the heartfelt stillness, You, O Lord, find rest, and we, as faithful people, discover peace, consolation and mercy.

Lord, since ancient days, You have welcomed us who thirst for You to come to the water and to satisfy our heartfelt thirst for You

Gift of Prayer

by our receiving Your divine counsel, guidance and justice. Lord, what can I do to bring You evermore into the lives of others? We are brothers and sisters and share in our humanity. We, as people, share in the imperfection and brokenness and frailties of our common humanity. Yet, so often, Lord, we, as people, fail to give ear and attention to You and Your divine counsel. Lord, in the stillness of the moment, I find time to listen as You whisper. Your Divine Word comes to me in words spoken by the frail, the elderly and the simple ones. It is in the stories of others' lives that I can discover You, O Lord. You speak and teach when I am still and, in that stillness, when I freely choose to pray and listen.

Lord, in the stillness of the early morning, as the dawn is breaking, and then in the quiet of the late-night hours, I search for You, O Lord. There, in those hours, You, O Lord, come to me. In the stillness of the hours, You shine forth. You are near. Even when I think You, O Lord, have abandoned me, I take heed, give You my ear, and then I discover that with great tenderness, You, O Lord, take hold of me and guide me throughout the coming hours. O Lord, my God, in the stillness of the day, You journey in my company. You call each person by name and bring us home to Your divine mercy, love and justice. Lord, let no one live a life void of Your presence; rather, with Your enduring love, have mercy upon those who are estranged or distant from You, our beloved Lord.

Lord, I shall not forsake You, I shall not grieve in Your absence, and I shall not forget You amid the imperfections of my humanity. You, O Lord, come into the lives of all who seek You. In the stillness of the human heart, You, Lord, find shelter, a holy temple and a cry for Your divine presence. Lord, sometimes You hide Your face from the very men, women and children who thirst for You. Why, I do not understand. Once You chose to walk in Eden with both Adam and Eve. Today, so many of us seek heartfelt stillness and Your presence, O Lord. Lord, we pray, we ask, we beseech You, dear Lord, to walk in our company. Lord, sometimes in the stillness of the day, I search for You and cannot find You. Still, Lord, I persevere in faith. I know You are near. After all, Your love, O Lord, will never leave the believer's heart.

Gift of Prayer

Lord, in the stillness of the moment, I have discovered that You bring good news, glad tidings and renewal to the faithful people. You, O Lord, bring redress and justice to those seeking forgiveness, mercy and reconciliation. Lord, Your beloved Son, Jesus Christ, died on that Cross for the sins of all people and nations. He rose on the third day to assure us that eternal life is ours for the asking. Lord, in every hour of every day, You, O Lord, hear the cries of countless human hearts. Lord, we voice our appeals, we silently pray with our petitions, and we joyfully await Your divine guidance, counsel and mercy. It is in the stillness of the moment that the Holy and Sacred impact our daily lives. It is then that the extraordinary becomes available to the ordinary. You, O Lord, linger in our crying hearts. You provide comfort, consolation, courage, strength, renewal and love. There amid the worries and fears of the human heart, You, dear Lord, assure us. You give ear to our petitions. In the stillness of day, You, O Lord, find refuge and attentive ears.

Lord, when the faithful gather together to worship and give You praise, we do so precisely because You are our God, and we are Your people!

Michael Briese

In the hush of those moments, in the silence of the day and amid the stillness of a prayerful heart, You, O Lord, find rest and stillness. There in those sacred and precious hearts, You, our Lord of divine mercy, justice and redemption, will find prayerful people: people who desire to know You more fully, people who desire to serve You more fully, and people who desire to make way for You. Lord, together, we cry out for You, and we shout with joy when You speak to us, guide us and inspire us. O Lord, our God, we share in that ancient covenant, and we desire ever more fully to love and serve You with all our heart and mind.

Lord, You call Your people to be attentive and to give ear to You. Lord, we are Your people, and we strive to listen as You speak. In the stillness of the day, we come before You, O Lord, our God. Lord, I cannot always know Your ways, but I can pray and strive to discern Your will. It is there in my prayers that I can discover Your divine counsel. You call us each by name, and we, in return, turn to You, O Lord. Lord, You invite us to hand our lives over to You, to allow our lives to be held in the palm of Your hand and to go out into the world with an awareness of You throughout the course of each passing day. Lord, we raise our eyes to heaven but realize You are with us here on earth. You wipe tears from our eyes, and we believe the day shall arrive when we see You face-to-face, and we shall discover eternal joy and peace.

Lord, Your beloved Son, our Lord Jesus Christ, died for all generations. We are Your people who have Your teaching at heart. Each day I awaken to Your divine gift of a breaking dawn, a new morning, a coming midday, an approaching evening and the expected late-night hours. Our Lord Jesus died and rose again for all generations: those who came before Him, those who were present when Jesus walked the earth and those who were to come after Him. Lord, in the stillness of the sacred moment, I can discover Your divine love and infinite mercy. I cannot fathom Your infinite love, but I can discern Your will. It is in the stillness of the day that I can find You, O Lord, my God.

Lord, I have stood amid the powers of hell, and Your divine love has prevailed! You, Lord, are our Lord of justice, mercy and love. Lord, during the stillness of the day, I have come to discover that You created the vast deserts, the immense waterways, the mountains and valleys, and that You, O Lord, even created the fish in the waters, the many animals in the forests and the countless birds that fly amid the heavens. Throughout Your creation, You, O Lord, make known Your presence. Lord, in stillness, I cannot forget You. O Lord, You are our maker, the One who stretched out the heavens and laid out the foundation of the earth. O Lord, Your presence is all around us. How can we miss You? Of course, if we do not look, we will not find. If we do not believe, we will never know You, our merciful and just God.

Lord, You ask us to trust in You. We pray and turn to You for guidance, counsel and renewal. Lord, Your daily presence is a pure gift. Your divine mercy and justice are pure gifts. Your creation of each new generation of people is a pure gift. O Lord, we come before You, and we hear You call, and we gather together within Your shadow. You give us the length of each day, and in return, we freely choose to live our daily lives in accordance with Your Gospel. In the stillness of the day, You, dear Lord, surround us with Your immense and infinite love. Lord, Your love transforms broken lives, heals the injured, renews the human spirit and overcomes fear. We place our trust in You, O Lord. This is our faith, and it was the faith of the generations who came before us. It will be the faith of generations yet to come. You, O Lord, my God, are beyond human comprehension. You are greater than human reason. Lord, we place our trust in You as You choose to shield us in the shadow of Your hand.

Lord, through faith, You put words into my mouth: words that help to console the lonely, words of counsel for those who desire guidance, and words to comfort the afflicted. Your divine words echo throughout the countless conversations held each day. Your divine mercy reaches into the lives of the depressed, the injured and the estranged. Lord, You are present to all whose daily lives intertwine with Your divine guidance. Lord, during the stillness of the day, there comes the moment when the divine and human are at one. It is then, in those hallow moments of each day that the divine and human join in union. Whether it be by word or deed, You, O Lord, come into the lives of countless people.

Michael Briese

Lord, You tell us to listen and hear You as You guide us to be people of justice, mercy and compassion. We hear You, O Lord, and we take Your holy words to heart. Let us rejoice and be glad! Let us go out each day and be modern disciples of our beloved Lord Jesus Christ. Let us bring love where once there was despair. Let us bring hope where once there was only desperation. Let us bring faith where once there was only doubt. Let us always cherish that stillness which rests within a faithful heart. Let us be people of God, whose words and deeds and daily lives bring the love of God into the lives of others. Let us be people who treasure God's immense love and countless gifts. Let us be people whose deepest desire is to love and serve our good and gracious Lord. In stillness, we pray. In stillness, we live out our lives and in stillness, we find our Lord as He rests within the temple of our faith-filled hearts. We trust in the name of our Lord and rely on His sacred words, His guidance and His immense love. Lord, have pity upon Your people and always journey in our company because You are our God, and we are Your people.

A SOLITARY HEART

O Lord, my God, I have that heartfelt desire to enter more fully into Your company. I seek to follow in the footsteps of Your beloved Son, our Savior Jesus Christ. Lord, my heart wrestles with Your angels; yet, I strive to remain attentive to You. I strive to live my daily life in accordance with the wisdom of the Holy Spirit. Lord, as I pray, I seek to listen to You and then to go out into the world and try to live each day by Your will, not my own will. Still, I fall way short all too often. Nonetheless, I persist!

Lord, Your test of any human being is but a mere taste of Your infinite divine mercy. Holy are You, dear Lord. I am humbled by Your immense mercy, justice and compassion. During the moments when evening has arrived, and as night is about to settle in, I am humbly able and willing to discover and obtain blessed spiritual renewal. Holy are You!

Michael Briese

I fear not the darkness of the night, the silence which permeates a solitary heart or walking a lifelong journey. I fear not the victory of the snare nor the power of evil. I know that, You, dear Lord, continue to guide and protect me. I wait in solitude, even during the darkness of the late-night hours. There in silence and with prayerful heartfelt attention, I can rediscover, recognize and humbly acknowledge You. May Your infinite gift of peace always prevail within the very depths of my being. In awe, I give thanks to You, O Lord, my God. Amen.

DEAR HOLY SPIRIT

I come before You in search of Your countless graces, blessings and wisdom. You bless each open heart, mind and spirit. You bless children with their innocence and genuine love. You bless teenagers with gifts of greater faith, greater hope and greater love. You bless young adults with greater knowledge, greater understanding and greater wisdom. You bless those who are middle age with a greater heartfelt awareness and understanding of Your divine mercy, heartfelt wisdom and the human need for greater justice. You bless those who are older with greater heartfelt faith, greater love and greater mercy. O Holy Spirit, Your spiritual presence is most clear in the hearts and lives of our dear and beloved, yet frail and somewhat forgetful elders. In the end, we pray You, dear Holy Spirit, will continue to permeate the very depth of our daily life. O, Holy Spirit, we deeply appreciate Your blessing us with our unearned gift of our one sacred, precious and holy lifetime. Dear Holy Spirit, in awe, we give thanks to You. AMEN.

PRAYER FOR THE ARMY OF PRAY-ERS

Lord, guide us with the wisdom of Your Holy Spirit. Enable us to enter ever more dearly into Your presence and to express our prayers to You, our Creator, Your only begotten Son and our Savior, Jesus Christ, and Your Holy Spirit of infinite divine love, mercy and justice. Teach us the art and power of prayer. Lord, grant us the courage to fold together our two hands and, ever so quietly within the very depths of our being, to most dearly lift up our prayers to You via our heartfelt cries, groans and whispers. There, in that moment of prayer, our heart and Your Spirit join in union to express and hear the cries of all Pray-ers. You even hear the prayers of those who intimately understand the heartfelt poverty of spirit. In the midst of such poverty, You, Lord, grant favor and greater compassion into wounded lives, broken hearts and suffering

Gift of Prayer

minds. You grant us solace and trust only You, dear Lord, can extend to another. We ask You, we beseech You, dear Lord, to ever more closely enter into our own lives, but also into the all too many lives in which heartfelt peace is a stranger, or, at best, a distant concept. Lord, we humbly lift up our hearts, minds, spirits and daily lives to You, our dear Lord. We do so at the behest and with encouragement from Your Holy Child, our Lord and Savior Jesus Christ. For this, we give thanks to You, O God! Amen.

PRAYER OF SUPPORT FOR STUDENTS AND YOUNG ADULTS

May their lives be blessed with many graces, God's wisdom, greater faith, true courage, renewal in spirit, sheer determination and perseverance. May they be blessed with a heart filled with hope and a willingness to learn, to give unto others, to help build up our society and to possess a greater awareness that, indeed, there rests within them an abundance of God's greatest gift—that of love. May our young people continue to grow as modern-day disciples of Christ.

We pray to the Lord . . .

PRAYER FOR VETERANS

Lord, we ask You to bring healing, renewal and encouragement to our veterans. They have spent precious parts of their lives striving to protect our nation, our homeland and our democratic way of life. We give thanks for all our veterans. They have given in ways immeasurable and invaluable: ways in which they cannot be adequately paid. We most especially give pause and prayer to those who have been injured or maimed in war. May our nation and its peoples always be there to serve and assist those who have suffered for us. Lastly, in deep awe, we give God our heartfelt thanks for those who gave the greatest sacrifice . . . their lives . . . in the name of our great country. With all the patriots our one nation under God remains indivisible with justice for all. Lord, again, we give thanks to You and all of our veterans. Amen.

PRAYER FOR FARMERS

Father, You are the Creator of all that is. You created the birds of the air, the vast waterways which stretch across Your great earthly domain, Your heavenly rains, the stars of the heavens, the ample forests, the countless creatures which roam the lands, the many fishes of the seas and most important, the many sacred and precious human lives which inhabit Your earth. Father, we give You thanks. Only with Your creation can the farmers of our world strive to till Your soil, plant Your seeds, sow Your vast creation of crops and experience Your provision of bountiful harvests. O God, our Creator, Your willingness to share the land and natural resources reminds us that we are to share the crops of the fields, the countless fruits of Your creation and, of course, the abundant natural resources only You can create.

Gift of Prayer

O Lord, grant your farmers a great trust in You. Remind our farmers as they stand in their fertile fields that only with You can they succeed in their farming endeavors. May Your farmers humbly come before You, O Lord, and acknowledge Your divine beauty which You entrust unto a farmer's stewardship. We give thanks to You, O Lord, for Your ancient divine wisdom and guidance. As stewards of Your creation, entrusted by You, O Lord, may we always be people whose hearts are reminded about Your daily care for us, our farms and the countless crops of the fields. We offer this prayer for farmers in a humble spirit of awe and thanksgiving.

PRAYER FOR PRIESTS

Our Father in heaven, we pray You will continue to watch over, guide, and protect our priests and bishops. We ask You, dear Lord, to hear their prayers, the cries of their heart and their heartfelt desire to more fully grasp Your hands. You are our Good Shepherd. You Lord humbly walk in the company of Your priests. We give thanks to You, and we ask You, O Lord, to awaken our lives and bless us with greater faith, greater hope and greater love. We plead You will always protect us from the snares of the wicked, temptations from fools and the countless sins of which we ourselves are quite capable. Lord, we give You praise for Your love, mercy, forgiveness and countless blessings. You Lord are our true Creator. All Glory and Honor is Yours as we give thanks and praise to You, dear Lord. Dearly beloved Father, Savior and Holy Spirit, in humble gratitude and deep awe we give thanks to You for our holy priesthood. We give praise to You who live and reign forever and ever. AMEN.

PRAYER FOR ADDICTS

by Reinhold Niebuhr

God, grant me the serenity to accept the things I cannot change, Courage to change the things I can, And wisdom to know the difference.

POPE FRANCIS'S MODERN BEATITUDES

Blessed are those who remain faithful while enduring evils inflicted on them by others and forgive them from their heart.

Blessed are those who look into the eyes of the abandoned and marginalized and show them their closeness.

Blessed are those who see God in every person and strive to make others also discover Him.

Blessed are those who renounce their own comfort in order to help others.

Blessed are those who pray and work for full communion between Christians.

THE BEATITUDES

"Blessed are the poor in spirit, for theirs is the kingdom of heaven.

Blessed are they who mourn, for they will be comforted.

Blessed are the meek, for they will inherit the land.

Blessed are they who hunger and thirst for righteousness, for they will be satisfied.

Blessed are the merciful, for they will be shown mercy.

Blessed are the clean of heart, for they will see God.

Blessed are the peacemakers, for they will be called children of God.

Michael Briese

Blessed are they who are persecuted
for the sake of righteousness, for theirs
is the kingdom of heaven.

Blessed are you when they insult you
and persecute you and utter every kind
of evil against you [falsely] because
of me.

Rejoice and be glad, for your reward will
be great in heaven. Thus they persecuted
the prophets who were before you."

(Mt 5:3–12)

THE BEATITUDES AS PRAYER

Lord, teach me to recognize You in the company of the least among us. Enable me to discover You in lives burdened by ill health or poverty. Lord, allow me to see Your presence in the company of those who are lowly and vulnerable. Lord, I ask You to make me worthy to see You in the lives of the frail, elderly, and disabled; those whose lives that are often blessed with purity of heart. O Lord, You permit me to choose freely... Remind me to LOOK! My God, You teach me to look around and see and discover Christ. Lord, You remind my prayerful heart to search always for You and that through others, especially the lowly, You continue to guide and speak to me. Since ancient days, You have told humanity that even the simple ones and the least among us have a story to tell. They too possess a dignity and a part in the unfolding of the Kingdom of God. Lord, I humbly pray that

Michael Briese

You, my dear Creator, will open my heart and mind to Your ways. Lord, encourage my heart to become more attentive, merciful, just and kind toward others.

O dear Lord, grant me the abilities, skills and gifts I need on a daily basis to live out Your sacred gift of this one lifetime. Lord, make me an instrument of Your Gospel. Guide me through this one holy, sacred and precious life as I strive to live out a devout life, a holy life and a life in imitation of You, our good and gracious Lord. Holy Father, I beg You to renew me and to enable me to imitate Your only begotten Son and our Lord, Jesus Christ. And may I, as a broken and imperfect human being, always strive to reach out in humble service to others and do what Christ would do. Lord, enable me to live out Your holy Gospel in both my words and actions. Lastly, I am grateful You taught me to read, reflect upon, pray over and live out THE BEATITUDES. O Lord, in a spirit of thanksgiving, I offer You this prayer with all my heart, all my mind and all my spirit. Amen.

WHO ARE MY NEIGHBORS

O Lord, I come into Your company in search of peace . . . that is, peace of heart, peace of mind and peace of spirit. I search, and still my heart remains restless. I strive to be attentive to You, my dearly beloved Lord. Yet, more so than not, I sense I am missing Your presence. I desire the heartfelt nourishment I find in the spiritual food of Your infinite divine love. Still, I know You have Your hands wrapped all around me. That, in itself, provides me with sufficient assurance. Lord, I know You are near. In knowing this I humbly give thanks to You, O Lord and God.

Lord, You sent forth Your only begotten Son, our Lord and Savior, Jesus Christ. Through my dearly beloved Savior, I know within the very depths of my being that my debt to You, dear Father, was settled long ago. Your Son paid the spiritual ransom needed to settle the account long ago. He came among mere human beings . . . men, women and children, and He walked in their company. Christ's message of forgiveness, redemption and eternal life was heard by many. Sadly, only some listened and freely chose to follow in His steps. Today, dear Lord, I wait in silence and, with greater clarity, I now more fully understand and humbly acknowledge my own realization that, like Christ, one day, You will send forth Your holy angels to carry me into Your eternal company. For this, I give thanks to You, my God. Holy are You, dear Lord.

As You bless me with every moment of life, every breath I take, every sunrise I witness and time itself, I, dear Lord, will strive to live a life in imitation of our Lord Jesus Christ. My dear Lord, as I approach the end of my lifelong race in the company of Christ, and as my journey draws me closer to its completion, I can only pray with great heartfelt desire to have lived a life about which You, my God, might genuinely acknowledge as being a life well lived and a journey well taken. I can only hope and pray that upon my final day, You, my dearly beloved Creator, will truly appreciate my own deeply

Gift of Prayer

flawed, frail and broken life. One day, I can only hope and pray this will be proven true.

Without You, my dear Lord, I am no one. I am a master at nothing, a mere fool walking along the face of this planet, and a man whose whole being is centered upon that ancient message of Your Holy Son, Jesus Christ. I guess I can truly say I have lived a fool's life, or might I say, a life of a man who was nothing more than a "fool for Christ." What a journey! What a life lived with a very deep daily awareness of just "how great thou art"! When Christ comes into my company, I know He is there and blesses me with greater heartfelt joy, greater peace and genuine happiness. My God, how great You are!

Lord, my neighbors remind me that You walk in the company of the least among us. Throughout most of my life, I have been willing and able to feed the hungry, give drink to the thirsty, provide clothes to the naked, and to visit the sick, the prisoner, a stranger in need, the widow and orphan and also to bury the dead. I have tried in my own imperfect ways to teach the ignorant, to provide good counsel to the doubtful, to admonish sinners, to bear wrongs patiently, to forgive those who trespass against me, to comfort the afflicted and to pray for the living and dead. I also strive to serve and pray for my neighbors, strangers and my friends and enemies.

Lord, what a life to live in words, prayers and actions! What a life! Hearts have been mended, minds brought greater awareness and change, and countless broken human spirits can now soar. Lives have been renewed and transformed. Marriages have been restored, strengthened, reconciled and sustained. Parents have opened their hearts and minds to children who once disappointed them. Strangers have risked their own reputations, even health and lives, in order to serve, safeguard, protect and strengthen others' lives.

You, dear Lord, were nailed to that ancient rugged Cross so that countless human lives might experience their own crucifixions and suffering, and, through their own passionate suffering, experience their own spiritual awakening, resurrection and a new sense of life itself. This is Christ's gift of a New Life—a spiritual life deeply embedded, and deliberately lived out, in the company of Christ.

This New Life in Christ is the divine gift about which the ancient prophets spoke, and for which countless believers waited in a spirit of expectation. This ancient gift of New Life in Christ brings with it spiritual fullness and greater knowledge, greater understanding and greater wisdom one can only hope to discover and live out in the company of Christ. In a spirit of deep awe, heartfelt love, and with a humbled heart, I give thanks to You, O dear Lord.

O Lord Jesus Christ, often I recognize You in the lives of my neighbors. I recall our Father's divine invitation as our Father encourages us to come closer, to draw near, to hear the Holy Word, and then to go out amid the darkness of the breaking dawn and to share with others the Good News lovingly bestowed upon the human race. For this divine invitation, I give thanks to You, my Lord. Holy are You, my Lord and my God. Amen.

GOLDEN ROSES

Lord, You blessed me with Your greatest gift—that of human life! Dear Lord, Your prophets assure humanity and stir our hearts and minds with Your countless blessings. Lord, Your divinely inspired and prayerful words reassure me, and hopefully all peoples, that my life and every human life is a holy life, a sacred life, and a precious life. Lord, You breathed into me and all humanity a lifetime of countless breaths, an abundance of Your holy moments, holy hours, holy days, holy seasons and holy years. My own human life was made holy at conception solely because You, dear Lord, granted me this most precious gift of human life. Thanks be to You, O Lord, my God. Holy are You, dear Lord, Holy are You.

Time and again You, dear Lord, granted me a Golden Rose. Throughout my lifetime, I have discovered this lifelong created bouquet of Your divine gifts. Your Golden Roses include, but are not limited to, my discovery, greater awareness and deeper heartfelt understanding that each Golden Rose represents You and Your infinite divine mercy, compassion and love. Lord, I cry within the very depths of my being when I realize it was You who granted unto me, Your unworthy servant, a lifetime of greater faith, greater hope and greater love.

O Lord, my God, why have You blessed me? What have I done to be worthy of You? Dear Lord, I humbly accept Your immense love, which is best exemplified by Your willingness to send forth Your only begotten Son, our Lord Jesus Christ, whose public suffering and death on that ancient Cross, when followed by His Resurrection, fulfilled the prophetic words foretold by the ancient prophets. Our Father in heaven, holy are You, our one true and dearly beloved Creator. Lord, You sent forth the wisdom of the Holy Spirit to bring rest, stillness and spiritual presence within the silence of my poor, broken and imperfect human heart. Lord, over all these passing years, You have blessed my life with an abundance of Golden Roses. Blessed are You, O Lord, our God Thanks be to You, dear Lord. AMEN.

O MOTHER MARY

O Mother Mary, may you continue to bless our lives as we journey in faith, hope and love. Be our model and guide us as we live in the grace won by your Son Jesus in his suffering and resurrection. May your motherly intercession for us bring healing, strength and renewal. O Mary, Mother of God, pray for us sinners. Help us to bring all people to your Son, especially those most in need of His mercy. May we grow in your image as disciples of Jesus. We pray this in His Holy Name. Amen.

HOLY MOTHER MARY

Holy Mother Mary, may you continue to bless lives deeply rooted in the faith, hope and love made possible by your suffering and resurrected Son, our Lord Jesus Christ. May lives be healed, strengthened and renewed as you, Holy Mary Mother of God, pray for us sinners. O Mother Mary, continue to guide countless hearts, minds and souls. Bless you, Holy Mary, Mother of God. Amen.

PRAYER FOR THE NEW YEAR

Lord, this New Year, teach me to follow in Your footsteps, to bring Your love into the lives of others, to feed the hungry, clothe the naked, visit the sick and the dying, care for the widow and orphan, help the stranger in need and serve the least among us. Lord, enable me to uphold the dignity of all people, including those who are weak, vulnerable and without a strong voice . . . most notably, the unborn and persons with disabilities. Lord, teach me to learn from the little ones. Teach me to see You through the lives of the poor in spirit and those whose lives are afflicted by addiction. Lord, bless me with the ability to hear Your heartfelt wisdom in the words of my elders, and the ill and suffering. Hear me, O Lord, and grant me the courage, perseverance and humility needed to imitate You. Lord, teach me to recognize You wherever I go. O Lord, guide me and bless me in ways everlasting. Lord, I ask You to grant this prayer. In peace, I humbly give thanks to You, my Lord and my God. Amen.

OH! ANCIENT NIGHT

Amid the stillness of that ancient night, while the world was in slumber, a child was born to a holy man and a blessed virgin. There in that manger was born a Holy Child. In His company were shepherds of the field, wise men and even animals. He grew up trained by and working with His father as a carpenter. At thirty years of age, this young Man went out to teach and preach, to forgive and heal and to die and rise. Since then, many empires have come and gone. So too have kings and armies and generations. He was a man whose simple but profound message of faith, hope and love continues to influence world history. He sought not fame, fortune nor power; rather, he humbly came with a message rooted in peace. In the end, this Carpenter has carved a new creation with a simple wish for peace on earth and goodwill to all.

OH! ANCIENT DAY

Mary's heart was broken. The apostles were in hiding. A guard stood near the tomb. The darkness of night surrendered to the breaking dawn, and red rays pierced the ancient sky. Dawn brought forth that ancient morning when time stopped, and human history was transformed by God Himself as He reached down into the tomb and raised up for us His Son Jesus Christ—The Light of the World.

The tomb was empty. Mary and the apostles ran to the empty tomb! They knew in their hearts and minds that the new day had brought forth the Risen Christ. Indeed, He had fulfilled the ancient words of the prophets. Death and its sting had been overcome by infinite divine love. Sin had been conquered by redemption and eternal life. Divine mercy had fallen upon humanity, and the human spirit was renewed by Hope.

Michael Briese

On that ancient morning, the Risen Light of the World brought forth the Good News. He had proclaimed freedom for prisoners, healing for the brokenhearted, hope for those in despair, forgiveness for all who choose to believe and reconciliation among enemies. Indeed, on that ancient day, morning had broken, the tomb was empty and the Light of the World had risen in New Life.

OH! GLORIOUS MOMENT

On that ancient day, in one glorious moment, He ascended into heaven and is now seated at the right hand of our Father. Born unto the Holy Virgin Mary and raised by His holy father Joseph, He walked among God's peoples. Scorned and rejected, He died on that old rugged Cross between two criminals. He was buried in a borrowed tomb. Three days later, He rose from the dead in fulfillment of the ancient prophets.

He had been crowned with thorns of glory and pierced with a soldier's lance. He brought forth redemption and the keys to the eternal city. He obtained the crowns of victory and divine mercy and justice. He brought glory to God in the highest, peace on earth, goodwill to all, reconciliation among enemies, hope in place of despair, faith for those who believe and salvation for sinners. In that one glorious moment, He ascended into heaven and now rests in the company of the angels and saints. He has been, is now and forever shall be the Savior of the world.

A PRAYER FOR PENTECOST

O Holy Spirit, I ask You to permeate the very depths of my being and to enter ever more deeply into my heart. O Holy Spirit, may You bring into our lives greater peace, deep awe, heartfelt appreciation and quiet rest amid life's turbulent waters. Bless Your disciples with Your holy and good counsel as we continue to discover, more fully understand and strive to imitate Your infinite divine mercy, wisdom and justice. Blessed Holy Spirit, I pray Your divine love is reflected in both my words and actions. I pray each day that Your eternal gifts of faith, hope and love are daily brought to life in and throughout countless lives. O God, our Father, may the Holy Spirit make all Your modern disciples steadfast sources of Your divine invitation. This You extend unto all peoples and nations. You encourage us to enter into and live out a more devout and holy life...a life deeply rooted in Jesus Christ. O Holy Spirit, may You continue to bless, strengthen and renew each and every human heart, mind and soul. Come, Holy Spirit, and continue to guide humanity through each unfolding day. This we ask in the Holy Name of our Redeemer and Savior Jesus Christ. Amen.

CORPUS CHRISTI SUNDAY PRAYER (BODY OF CHRIST)

O Lord, You granted to the holy apostles and our Church Your gift of Your Real Presence in our ancient Sacrament of Holy Eucharist. There, at the Last Supper shared on that first Holy Thursday, You took bread, broke it and gave it to the apostles. In that moment of human history, You enabled humanity to enter into an eternal relationship in which we can actually receive Your sacramental Real Presence. You invite and encourage us to freely receive Your one True and Real Presence through the Sacrament of Holy Communion. Lord, we thank You for Your willingness to enter into the Passion, and we marvel at that historic moment when humanity witnessed Your Crucifixion. Indeed, Lord, Your Crucifixion was followed by the fulfillment of the ancient prophets when You defeated death and resurrected from the dead. On that ancient day, You granted all who enter into Your company the ability to witness and share in the breaking of the Bread and the true Body of Christ. Through Holy Eucharist, we are able to receive and share Your Real Presence and the countless blessings You grant through our ancient Sacrament of Holy Eucharist. In Holy Eucharist, we witness the transubstantiation as man's harvested bread becomes Your actual sacred and precious Real Presence. Our one holy, Catholic and apostolic Church says "AMEN" as our expression of thanksgiving to You, our One, Most Holy Savior. Dear Lord, we give thanks to You for granting us this sacred gift and Your gifted promise of eternal life. In a spirit of humility, we give thanks to You, dear Lord. Amen.

PRAYER FOR DEACONS

"Receive the Gospel of Christ whose herald you now are. Believe what you read, teach what you believe and practice what you teach."

PRAYER FOR HEALING THROUGH FR. AL SCHWARTZ

O Father, I ask You for healing of my mind, body, soul and spirit. I do so through the prayers and intercession of the Venerable Father Al. I ask You, O Lord, to lift high my illness and to bring healing, renewal and greater faith and joy. I beseech You, O Lord, to hear my prayers and to sustain healing. I do so in the name of the Venerable Father Al and in the Holy Name of Jesus Christ. Amen.

MOTHER'S DAY BLESSING

Loving God, we thank You for the love of the mothers you have given to us, whose love is so precious that it can never be measured, and whose patience seems to have no end. Lord, may we see Your loving hand behind them and guiding them. We pray for mothers who might fear they will run out of love, time or patience. We pray for mothers who have gone before us. Lord, we ask You to bless all mothers with Your infinite and divine holy love. May Almighty God bless all mothers in the name of the Father, of the Son and of the Holy Spirit. Amen.

FATHER'S DAY BLESSING

Our Father who art in heaven, we ask you to bless our dear fathers, whose deepest expression of love helped to create the gift of our own human lives. They nourish our lives with daily bread, love and support. Dear Father, please bless each father's heart, mind and spirit. Bring them away from any temptation and help them to live good lives as they journey through this life in the company of the angels and saints. Dear beloved Father, please continue to grant our fathers heartfelt wisdom, divine mercy and goodness. We ask all this in the Holy Name of Your beloved Son Jesus Christ. Amen.

BLESSING FOR GRANDPARENTS

Lord, we ask You to bless all grandparents and keep them in Your care. Bless them with peace, health and healing. Reward them for their faith and fidelity, for their work and goodness, for their love and thoughtfulness, for their gifts and prayers. Give them a long and happy life. May the advancing of years come to them in the company of family and friends. We ask You to unite them again in the kingdom of Your love where parting will be no more. And may Almighty God bless all grandparents in the name of the Father, the Son and the Holy Spirit. We ask all this through Christ our Lord. Amen.

BLESSING FOR THOSE WHO HAVE DISABILITIES

Lord Jesus, You are the Healer, Holy Redeemer and Savior of humanity. When You walked among us, You brought healing to those among the least of us. Never did You refuse to heal, renew and bring forth God's infinite love.

Together, we as a community of believers ask You to bring healing and blessings to those who are blind and cannot see the rising of the sun as You stretch out Your divine hands and create each new day. They are blind to Your creative artworks of the many waterways, mountains and valleys and vast flowers and crops and forests. Yet, clearly they can see the face of God and live in Christ and follow in His footsteps.

Gift of Prayer

Lord, bring healing and renewal to the deaf who cannot hear the charming songs sung by the countless birds of the heavens. They cannot hear the roaring of the ocean waves. Still, because of Christ, they can hear You, O Lord, as You whisper within the silence of their hearts. There You whisper softly, and the many gifts of the Holy Spirit echo forth therein. Blessed is the person who comes closer to You, O Lord!

Lord, bless those whose minds are lost in the darkness of society. Bless them! Bless them! They have lost their abilities to think clearly, to reason and to discern. Some say they are crazy. Others say they are despondent, depressed and lost. You, O Lord, walk among them and bring to them the healing and stability only Your love can generate. Lord, rest within the very fiber of their hearts and minds. Bring them healing, stability and renewal.

Lord, there are those whose simplicity is admired and honored. Their hearts are so pure, so trusting and so virtuous. It is a challenge to find others whose lives so clearly remind us to search for, discover and live out a life deeply rooted in Your greatest gift of Love.

Michael Briese

O Lord, bless those whose human condition with all its frailties limit their mobility. Some are even bedridden. Lord, bless them with the ability and power to pray. They can be the Army of Pray-ers humanity so badly needs. Make them Your prayerful angels here on earth. Already, their lives are blessed, sacred and holy.

Remind us, O Lord, that our good health is filled with blessings. Teach us to serve those among the less fortunate, to care for the sick and the dying. Allow us to be humbled by the quiet, steadfast courage and persistence of those who suffer. Teach us to be humbled by their faith and daily lives. In the end, make us lovers of others . . . especially those among the frail, sick and vulnerable in society.

Lord, often You come face-to-face with us when we are open to the simple words of a sick person, a trusting child or a suffering soul. It is then we see You face-to-face, and we discover joy! You shelter us, protect us and teach us. You wipe away our tears and bring us joy and renewal. Hear us, O Lord, and rest in our company.

QUEENSHIP OF THE BLESSED VIRGIN MARY

Holy Queen, Mother of God, we petition you to watch over and guide us. We ask you to watch over our hearts, minds and souls and protect them from the various temptations we can experience in life.

Blessed Virgin Mary, we ask you to bestow upon our Church, our community and our nation a greater sense of mutual respect for one another.

Holy Mary, Mother of God, help to guide us and enable us to imitate Christ by your virtues and by living out the Christian life.

Mother of Christ, remind us daily to make time to pray for our Church and our nation, to pray the Rosary and to regularly receive Holy Communion.

We pray for all those who have suffered this past year. For them and their loved ones, we pray for healing, renewal, improved spirits and greater faith.

We pray for those and all who have died in this last year, that they may experience the fullness of True Salvation and find great peace and comfort in the company of our Lord and Savior Jesus Christ and all the angels and saints.

Lord, we give thanks to You for Your infinite love, divine mercy, holy redemption and salvation.

Father, in the name of the Blessed Queen and Virgin Mother Mary, we offer You these prayers and those within the silence of our hearts in the Holy Name of Your beloved Son, our Savior Jesus Christ. Amen.

FINAL BLESSING

Bow your heads and pray for God's blessing.

Lord, help your people to seek you with all their hearts

And to deserve what you promise.

Grant this through Christ our Lord. Amen.

May Almighty God bless you,
The Father, and the Son and the Holy Spirit. Amen.

A PRAYER

God Almighty, guide us each day. Open our hearts to the loving wisdom of your holy spirit. Open our minds to the greatest act of love Brought to us through the Redemptions of Your Son, Jesus Christ. Open our ears so we may hear your Words and listen attentively to the words of others. Bless our words so that our mouths may bring the good news into the daily lives of others, Teach us Lord to pray mire, to be patient, and to realize that your love guides us on the daily pathway to peace.

PRAYER I

Prayer is the language of the human heart. Prayer can be expressed in the silence of a late night when one's heart cries out using no oral words. Our Lord knows more fully than you or me that prayer is, in fact, the silent cries deeply embedded in the very depth of one's self. Prayer is that great expression we can experience within the human spirit which rests in the depth of one's being. There inside you is a temple for our dearly beloved Lord. There within that very silence rests the Eternal One. Our spiritual vision is noted in St. Paul's words, "At present we see indistinctly, as in a mirror, but then face to face. At present I know partially; then I shall know fully, as I am fully known" (1 Cor 13:12). Our Lord finds rest, goodwill, courage and steadfast faith within the abiding heartfelt faith you have been granted. Treasure this divine presence within your own heart, mind and spirit.

Michael Briese

Our Lord is with you and all who are in search of our Lord's immense love, divine mercy and daily presence. Go off to a quiet place and there welcome our dearly beloved Lord. Do so in silence, with heartfelt love, childlike trust and blessed wonder. Wonder and you will find wisdom. Pray and you will see God. Then in deep heartfelt humility, give thanks to our one common Creator. Lastly, in a spirit of awe, allow your heart to express deep gratitude to He who walks in your company.

Prayer is for you, and, I personally believe, is for all people living on this great planet of Earth. If you are willing to pursue a great education, or to study, work in a trade, and over some years, learn and become a skilled craftsman; or if you are skilled at managing the resources of the earth, the seasonal rains and snows, and the crops of the fields, then you too have recognized God's various gifts. He provides countless crops of the fields, the various flowers in the gardens, the many animals of the forests, the herds of livestock, the countless trees of the forests and the various fishes of the ample waterways on earth . . .

Gift of Prayer

If you can develop your mind, your abilities and your own personal sinew, then you, in fact, will have lived your one life using the gifts God granted you. Realize God's countless gifts granted to your family members, the neighbors nearby, the strangers you might meet, and even to your enemy . . . These are all ways in which God speaks daily. If you do not look, you will not see. If you do not listen, you will not hear. If you think you have done all this on your own, take a hard look at truth! You owe yourself truth! God encourages all of us to live our lives as it is written in Hebrews 4:16, "So let us confidently approach the throne of grace to receive mercy and to find grace for timely help." Our Lord hears you! Do you give ear to our Lord and listen with an attentive heart, mind and spirit? Hear these sacred words of divine assurance, ". . . And behold, I am with you always, until the end of the age" (Mt 28:20).

Our dear Lord always reminds you, me and all humanity that we are to be forgivers. We are to let go of the past. Close yesterday's door and move forward. Our Lord spoke through St. Paul when he wrote, "[And] be kind to one another, compassionate, forgiving one another as God has forgiven you in Christ" (Eph 4:32). Prayer is that breath you take, that step you take, that ability to witness yet another sunrise or sunset. You are so blessed. Your life is already holy precisely because God willed your creation and has a place for you in the unfolding of His kingdom here at hand. Have the courage to place your life into the outstretched hands of our Lord. Go off to that place where the sacred can quietly enter into the temple of your frail, broken and imperfect heart. Go off to that place in God's creation where you and our dear Lord can enter into a spiritual union, a place and moment when man and God are indeed aware of each other's presence. There you will discover and rediscover our Lord's presence within the very fibers of your own holy life. Trust in our dear Lord and know, "Fear of the LORD is the beginning of knowledge; fools despise wisdom and discipline." "The beginning of wisdom is fear of the LORD, and knowledge of the Holy One is understanding" (Prv 1:7; 9:10).

Listen to our dear Lord throughout the passing of each hour every day. Pray and pray more. When you doubt whether your prayers are real, sincere or have any real value, then that kind of reflection, wonder and careful self-examination is the beginning of a prayer life in which life itself will keep you closer to our dear Lord. Also, you will grow over your lifetime in your keen and attentive awareness of our Lord's impact on you and the holy life you sincerely seek to live . . . one hour, one day at a time. "The LORD answered: I myself will go along, to give you rest" (Ex 33:14).

My dear brothers and sisters in Christ, "Do not conform yourselves to this age but be transformed by the renewal of your mind, that you may discern what is the will of God, what is good and pleasing and perfect" (Rom 12:2). Always be sincere. Do not try to play some role as a disciple of Christ. That is just acting. Rather, be a person of perseverance, determination and courage. If you truly are seeking to spend a lifetime in the company of Christ, then, like Christ, you must be willing to experience the rejection, slander, lies, cheating and so much more of the negativity which is part of our community. Even those who exhibit these behavoirs are children of God. And they, like you, were brought into this world as children of God. But do they listen to our dear Lord?

Michael Briese

Accept a person as they are. Greet them with sincere kindness. Be present to another person. "Rejoice with those who rejoice, weep with those who weep" (Rom 12:15). Like Christ, and as a human being bearing genuine brokenness, imperfection and doubts, read these sacred words, "Because he himself was tested through what he suffered, he is able to help those who are being tested" (Heb 2:18).

In 1 John 3:17–18, it is written, "If someone who has worldly means sees a brother in need and refuses him compassion, how can the love of God remain in him? Children, let us love not in word or speech but in deed and truth." Luke also reminds us that a holy life in Christ should seek and be willing to, "Give and gifts will be given to you; a good measure, packed together, shaken down, and overflowing, will be poured into your lap. For the measure with which you measure will in return be measured out to you" (Lk 6:38).

Whatever you choose to pursue in this gift of one lifetime, I pray you will freely choose to put Christ first. This life will not always be easy. Ironically, sometimes the biggest burdens you must bear will be placed upon your frail shoulders by people who do not necessarily care much about you, or anyone else. They can often appear to be tough, nasty people. Maybe they are; but, again, we must always remind ourselves and one another, as well as these same people, that their own life is, in fact, sacred, precious and holy. This is precisely because God has created them out of divine love and in His image and likeness, and they have a role to play in the unfolding of God's Kingdom here at hand. Even the least among us have goodness within. Recognize this always.

Remind them about their own sacred life and about the goodness they have possessed since that holy day and holy moment when God breathed life into them. Ask them if they even know this. Ask them, "HOW do you give back to our Lord?" When you either freely choose or must walk among people who are liars and cheaters, be attentive, listen to what might not be said, to the way in which words are spoken, and, of course, the words themselves. Look right into the eyes of whoever is speaking to you. Listen! Listen! Do all this in the Holy Name of Jesus, and you will have fulfilled these sacred words, "Those who go forth weeping, carrying sacks of seed, Will return with cries of joy, carrying their bundled sheaves" (Ps 126:6). "Softer than butter is his speech, but war is in his heart. Smoother than oil are his words, but they are unsheathed swords" (Ps 55:22). "And over all these put on love, that is, the bond of perfection" (Col 3:14).

In the end, all you can do is meet a person where they are, give them your best efforts and allow our Lord to speak to you through the least among us. You will fail far more often than you will succeed. The key to successfully living out a life centered on Christ is not measured by an average or numbers; rather, success is when you humbly seek to follow in the footsteps of our beloved Lord, Jesus Christ. That deep, genuine, heartfelt desire in itself is God's ample graces and blessings and heartfelt wisdom shining forth into a place and moment when you, as a modern disciple of Christ, brought forth His Good News in a spirit of service deeply rooted in the greatest gift—that of love.

If you have done your best, even amid defeat, simply end that day keenly aware our

Gift of Prayer

good Lord is with you now and until the hour of your death. Then in prayer, trust and a spirit of thanksgiving, place your head upon a pillow and believe you will be granted a new day. Be at peace with the world, God and yourself, and seek rest and renewal.

PRAYER II

With prayerful eyes and ears we turn to our Lord and ask that we may be blessed in faith and in prayer. We pray that we may be able to discern God's will, that our desire to more fully grasp and know God will be granted, and that we may be granted the gifts with which we can grow in virtues, prayer, and holiness. O Lord, our God, You give us faith to enlighten our minds, open our hearts, and renew our lives. Lord, I ask You to journey in my company all the days of my life. I ask You to give light where there is only darkness, direction where there is but distraction, and trust where once there was only doubt. O Lord, our God, come into the depths of all whose hearts cry out to You. You hear the cries of the poor, the sick, the lost, and those who are paralyzed in disbelief. O Lord, amid the darkness of the human heart, we can in fact come to rest in the presence of You, our good and gracious Lord. You are at once present to us and yet by nature, You are beyond the human realm. Lord, You grant us a prayerful spirit and as such, we can often see, even amid the blindness or darkness of our own hearts. Lord, through prayer we can see, hear, listen and come to discern Your will. Lord, when we pray, we ask for Your steadfast guidance, counsel, and renewal.

Lord, I come before You as a person of prayer who struggles even with grace, faith, and hope. I am like a beggar who comes before You. I am unworthy to tie Your shoe, to be in Your divine presence, or to beg from You. I am an unworthy servant whose heart cries out for Your divine blessings and presence. It is in prayer that I am a beggar who stands in Your company. I cry out in prayer and You, dear Lord, hear the sound of my cry. It is at that moment during my cries that a human being and You, the Divine One, stand in union. In that moment of prayer, humanity and God are willing to listen to one another. In that moment there is a mutual willingness to see and understand one another with the sight and discernment rooted in a faithful heart and divine love. This can be a sacred time, a biblical moment, a time when God and human are one. Such intimate prayer is the gift from God that teaches us to be humble and willing to place our vulnerable selves into God's open hands. Prayer can be that experience when human love and divine love will be in union.

O Lord, what can I learn from a devout life, a life of faith, hope, and love, and a life lived in Your divine presence? Lord, take me by my hand, guide me and teach me to walk daily in Your holy company. Lord, teach me to think truth with my heart, to see with a prayerful disposition, to walk in a spirit of justice, and to pray with the simple trust of a child. Lord, teach me to listen to my heart, to avoid being judgmental or gossipy, and enable me to see Your divine strength even in the midst of human weakness, foibles, or brokenness. Lord, I cannot count the ways in which You choose to guide us in prayer.

O Lord, I ask You to teach me more and more about the ways in which I can freely choose to love others, including my neighbor, the stranger, or even my enemy. My dearly beloved Lord, only through prayer can I hope to come to a greater understanding about You.

Gift of Prayer

Only through prayer can I hope to be more loving, more just, and more faithful. Only through prayer can I hope to see the divine among humanity. Lord, You have so much to teach that even the faith of a beggar can be replenished.

Lord, as people we need to step back from the daily schedule, to take time to pray and listen to You, and we need to be willing to discern Your divine will. We need to truly hand over ourselves, our lives, and our very being to You, O Lord. The questions to ask include, "Are we willing to do this?" "Are we willing to come before our good and gracious Lord and ask, beg for His divine counsel, healing, or guidance?" and "Do we gather in the company of the faithful in search of God's mercy and love?" O God, my God, in You I find comfort and refuge. In Your company I find greater understanding and wisdom. Lord, through prayer I speak and listen to Your divine guidance and counsel. You are our God and we are Your people!

Lord, since Adam we have realized that all people are created in Your image and likeness. We believe the dignity of each person is firmly rooted in Your love. We see Adam as being our common thread to You, our divine Creator. The dignity of every person is to be recognized whether one is a millionaire or beggar, wise leader or humble servant, famous or unknown. We believe this! However, we recognize the signs of God are all around us. Prayer is the avenue that opens up the human heart to Your divine will, Your divine wisdom, and Your divine justice. O Lord, teach us to pray and to pray more.

Lord, we pray, we ask that You give us the eyes to see and the ears to hear as You speak to us throughout each day. Lord, when we take the time to look around we might see an infant, an elderly person, a street person, or a successful person in business attire. When we see these and other people, we need to recognize and realize that we are looking at people created in God's image and likeness. O Lord, my God, in prayer I give thanks to You. With all my heart I turn to You, O Lord. Without fear I declare Your wondrous deeds and point out Your presence here among us. O Lord, my God, You are at once beyond my station in life and also a servant whose humility is the model to imitate. O Lord,

Gift of Prayer

the poor, the afflicted, the lost all cry out for You. On You we depend, and we turn to You for healing and renewal. Prayer is the way that You, our Lord, give us direction and countless gifts.

O Lord, deep within our prayerful hearts are desire and a longing for You. We hunger, we thirst for a deeper relationship with You, our Almighty One. Lord, You sent Your only begotten Son, our Lord Jesus Christ, to preach and teach, to heal and counsel, and to die and rise from the dead. There can be no mistaking Your divine love, redemption or justice. Your only Son walked among saints and sinners. By dying on that ancient cross and rising from the dead, Jesus gave us a moment when human history was turned upside down. It was a moment when You, O Lord, heard the cries of countless hearts and minds and generations from the past, the present and the future. At that moment, You, dear God, and humanity were as one. Today, we come before You, O Lord, and we discover in Jesus, the Son of a carpenter, Your divine presence. Prayer is the way of a faithful heart. Holy are You, O Lord, our God! Lord, we gather together in worship to give You thanks and praise. We come before You with alert spirits, and humble hearts and minds that desire to rest in Your presence. Prayer is the way we can speak and listen to You. O Lord, You willingly and out of love place into our hearts and minds that ancient God-given gift of faith. You nourish us with grace and counsel. You strengthen and renew our daily lives with hope and splendor. Lord, You are at once within the confines of a faithful heart and simultaneously beyond human history and time itself. Lord, Your gift of hope sharpens our prayers. Hope is made by You, given by You and nourished by You, our God. With hope come blessings and joy. We experience joy when we give You honor and thanksgiving for all You have done, are doing, and will do in the future. You, O Lord, bless us with hope and joy, which rest within the deep chambers of our prayerful hearts.

Lord, prayer brings delight to those who savor Your daily presence. Prayer is the avenue by which Your teachings and grace can foster greater faith, hope, and love. Lord, when I pray, I strive to discern Your counsel and ways. You are our Lord and Creator. We are here but for a short time. We are to spend our lives in search of You and when we find You, we are to live our lives in accordance with Your ways. O Lord, You hear our prayers at dawn, in the afternoon, in the evening hours, and during the darkness of night. Lord, no time is beyond You. You hear our cries and petitions at whatever moment we decide to turn to You in prayer. Lord, You have been, are, and ever shall be, until the end of the ages, until there is no tomorrow, and until the end of eternity. Lord, all time is Your time! We come before You in prayer asking for Your guidance and blessings as we journey through the number of years You grant to each one of us.

Lord, when I call on You, answer me, for You are my just and merciful Lord. My prayers are the cries of my inward temple, my heart, and my mind. There in the silence of the moment I can pray and discern Your will. Lord, You look beyond the limitations of my prayerful words. You see what I cannot see. You understand well beyond my human limitations. Lord, You know my heart better than I know myself. Lord, when I cry out in prayer, You realize that I cannot speak or pray the countless prayers and petitions resting in the silence of my human heart. O Lord, hear my cries and hear also the cries I cannot know or hear. Lord, bless me with Your divine guidance and give me the understanding of Your divine counsel. This is my prayer. This I ask of You, O God.

Hear my cries, O Lord, and attend to my worries and concerns. Hear the whispers that echo in the chambers of my soul. Bless me with the stillness needed to pray, and bless me with an attentive heart and a listening mind. Teach me, Lord, to go beyond the limitations of myself. Guide me in Your everlasting path. Make known to me the wisdom of a prayerful heart and mind. O Lord, to You I pray. Through Your abundant kindness and mercy, we are able to enter into Your presence. You create holy vessels out of our lives and holy temples within the silence of the human heart. O Lord, my God, I seek to surrender my prayerful self to Your divine ways. Your guidance is a beacon shining within the hopeless days of many past lives. You bring forth spiritual courage, renewal, and maturity. Lord, Your ways are our ways and Your kingdom is among us. Now, Lord, we gather in Your divine presence in search of that eternal day when time itself will be no more and eternal life shall be ours. O God, my God,

Gift of Prayer

You create us out of love and in Your image and likeness. You sent Your only Son to die on that cross and to rise again in order to bring us eternal life. Now, at this moment, as time is passing, as prayers are being said, and as lives are filled with Your infinite love and grace and justice, let us pray that You, O Lord, will always walk in our company. This we ask in Christ's name.

PRAYER III[*]

Prayer is the road map we use to express our deepest heartfelt desires, hopes, and cries for help. Why pray? Precisely because prayer is the cry of a broken heart, a humbled spirit, a dejected stranger in need, the neighbor in despair, or even the wails of an upset child. Prayer transcends human limitations and breaks through whatever earthly limitations we must confront. Prayer is the language of a human heart in search of the Divine. Prayer transcends our own human nature and takes our deepest heartfelt cries and prayers up into the heavens where our Lord patiently waits. In turn, the wisdom of the angels brings blessings to us. We receive guidance, counsel, and wisdom. God Himself blesses us, renews us, guides us, and strengthens our God-given gifts of faith, hope, and love. Prayer is the bridge

---

[*]Prayer from *Spiritual Common Sense* by Michael Briese, pages 43–53.

that connects the human with the Divine. Prayer is one of the greatest resources we have as human beings. Prayer brings healing, reconciliation, forgiveness, renewal, strength, greater knowledge, greater understanding, and greater wisdom. Prayer is God's great gift. All you need to do is have an open heart, an open mind, and soul. Renewal shall be yours for the asking. Pray and you shall encounter our good and gracious Lord.

Pray throughout each and every day. If you can, set aside some time (maybe fifteen minutes) each morning and read Holy Scripture and pray. In the late morning hours, find two or three minutes to give for simple quiet prayer. Then in the late afternoon, find another three minutes to reflect and pray about the passing day. Then, in the evening or later at night, take fifteen minutes to read Holy Scripture, pray, reflect, and find stillness. At the end of the day, as you place your head on the pillow, give thanks to the Lord and go and find peace and rest.

In prayer, awaken to the sunrise and be stunned by the fabulous, almost miraculous creation of each and every breaking dawn. Our

Michael Briese

Lord hears our cries and prayers and grants us each a new day. The psalmist wrote, "This is the day the Lord has made; let us rejoice in it and be glad" (Ps 118:24). In our modern days, we often overlook the obvious signs of God's infinite and impressive gifts!

Prayer is the avenue we journey in our daily spiritual search for our Lord and Savior Jesus Christ. God's providential concern and care for humanity is most evident when we realize and humbly acknowledge that every breath we take comes from God. After all, when God so wills that we return home, then we shall take our last breath and return to the eternal life. How many breaths has God granted unto you in your lifetime? Millions? Billions? Trillions? What did you do to earn or deserve this lifetime? Probably nothing! Still, in prayer we are humbly impressed by God's immense love. Then, in prayer we give thanks to our Lord.

Through prayer, we learn that God loves us. He grants us every moment of every day of every month, of every year throughout our lifetime. Time never ceases. Recognize that every hour is a holy hour and every day a holy day, precisely because all time is God's time and human history is but a part of God's eternity. Though we will die and our human life will come to an end in human history, it is also important to recognize that our spiritual journey continues through God's eternity.

Time is an answer to many prayers, as lives are lost, broken, forgotten, and as such, a spiritual search for our Lord begins with prayer. Pray and pray more. There is never enough prayer or too much prayer. When you cannot think or speak the cries of your heart, or the despair in your mind or body, then simply and humbly come before our Lord and ask Him to relieve you of your spiritual burdens. Ask and our Lord will hear you.

Praying without ceasing is a real challenge. But, prayer can become as natural as one's breathing. Pray as you awaken each morning. Amid any hectic rush in the morning with regard to children, school, or work responsibilities, find time, make time to pray. After all, God is always watching us, waiting in our company, and willing to grant us guidance, wisdom, and many graces. Pray and pray more. Matthew writes, "'Ask and it will be given to you; seek and you will find; knock and the door will be opened to you'" (Mt 7:7). John writes, "'Until now you have not asked anything in my name; ask and you will receive, so that your joy may be complete'" (John 16:24). Prayer is the passionate cries of a thirsting heart. When you thirst for the Lord, go off to a quiet place, find stillness and silence, and then quietly give thanks to our God.

Prayer is not always easy. Sometimes we can be very hard and very critical of our own spiritual journey. We can become stubborn or egotistic or unwilling to change. Still, our Lord waits patiently for you and me. God waits and waits. He is always with us. Know your true self! John in his first letter writes, "Beloved, if [our] hearts do not condemn us, we have confidence in God and receive from him whatever we ask, because we keep his commandments and do what pleases him." (1 John 3:21–22). Pray and always persevere. Trust in our Lord, knowing full well that our Lord is with us now and until the end of time!

Whether one is poor or wealthy, well or poorly educated, powerful or weak, blessed

Gift of Prayer

with fame or simply unknown, or blessed with faith or lacking in faith, our Father sent His only begotten Son to die and rise for all peoples of all nations, of all times. Know that God Himself invites you to come home to the waiting Son whose outstretched hands are ready to hug and renew and strengthen you. Go forth amid doubts, uncertainty, a lack of clarity, or mystery and walk humbly in the company of Christ. Prayer is this healing and forgiving and unifying process. Join in with the faithful and come home to our Lord!

God is always with us and willing to hear our prayerful words and cries. We are in the eyes of the Divine. God knows who we are better than we know ourselves. Spiritually, we grow only over the years, as we are willing to be formed by our Lord. He molds our sinful life into a life of prayer, mercy, and justice. Over the years, sinners are transformed into holy men and women, people who are prayerful and willing to live their lives in accord with God's will. A psalmist wrote, "O just God, | who tries hearts and minds" (Ps 7:10). Also, it is written, "The Lord knows the plans of man; | they are like a fleeting breath" (Ps 94:11). A psalmist also wrote, "you understand my thoughts from afar" (Ps 139:2). Since ancient days, believers have constantly realized God's immense love and mercy and God's constant presence in our midst. Prayers can bring us many blessings, greater knowledge, more complete spiritual understanding, and an abundance of God's heartfelt wisdom. Prayer is the language of the human heart!

Some might say prayer is a longing, a thirst, a deep desire to come closer to our Lord. Prayer might also be described as being like a ladder in that we slowly climb up the spiritual ladder one step at a time. Prayer is an ongoing process in which we spiritually first learn to crawl, then walk, and then run. But even those who can run the spiritual race trip and fall. Then they must get back up and persevere in their spiritual formation and prayer life. No one does this without some hard work and constant efforts. Prayer forms the very depths of our being precisely because prayer demands much from us. And this we do all for the sake of our relationship with our Savior and loving Lord Jesus Christ. The Scripture says "But the one who perseveres to the end will be saved" (Mt 24:13). Pray without ceasing.

Gift of Prayer

In prayer, pray with a deep and genuine love for our Lord. Pray in love and you will grow in love. Pray with faith and certitude and trust and you will grow and mature in your relationship with our Savior and His Father. Pray in ways that when you cease, you realize you are NOT praying. Stay close to our Lord with a prayerful heart, mind, and soul. See the sacred amid the ordinary, the holy right here in your midst and the handiwork of the Divine all around you. It is written, "Commit your way to the Lord;|trust in him and he will act" (Ps 37:5). And it is written, "Give thanks to the Lord, who is good, whose mercy endures forever" (Ps 106:1). In prayer, be humbled to stand before our Lord and to pray in the company of the saints and angels.

Prayer is supposed to be a conversation with our Lord. Sometimes people get too used to doing all the praying by doing all the talking. Well, slow down! And quiet down. Be still, and in that stillness come before our Lord and pray by being quiet and listening as our Lord whispers within the silence of your heart. It is written, "And we have this confidence in him, that if we ask anything according to his will, he hears us. And if we know that he hears us in regard to whatever we ask, we know that what we have asked him for is ours" (1 John 5:14–15). Learn to surrender your own words to silence. In prayer it is VERY true that "silence is golden." Go off to a quiet place, be still, and in silence listen in prayer. Listen!

If you are generally living a good and moral life, if you are trying to live a Christian life, and if you are putting your faith into action, then you are well on your way to living out the Gospel. In the ancient days, it was written, "[I]f then my people, upon whom my name has been pronounced, humble themselves and pray, and seek my face and turn from their evil ways, I will hear them from heaven and pardon their sins and heal their land" (2 Chr 7:14). Our Lord invites you to come closer, to fall so deeply in love with our Lord that you will forever be a faithful disciple of our Risen Lord Jesus Christ.

Sometimes people tell us more about who they are and where they are coming from in life by their words. Words are important. Words have meaning. Words can bring great joy, but words can also bring wounds. Prayer is always about speaking to the Holy and Almighty.

As such, prayerful words are important. It is written, "If you remain in me and my words remain in you, ask for whatever you want and it will be done for you" (John 15:7). Pray by speaking with a tender spirit. If you come to prayer in anger, then, calm down and be still and quiet and in that silence slow down and allow the Lord to speak to you. Sometimes silence speaks volumes. Listen in prayer.

For those who are just beginning to try to make sense of the prayer life, know our good and gracious Lord has a special place for you. You are at the start of a great lifelong and eternal adventure. The prayer life will help you to climb many ladders or mountains, to walk in darkness and to see a great Light! Be persistent in your prayer life. It is written, "But if any of you lacks wisdom, he should ask God who gives to all generously and ungrudgingly, and he will be given it" (James 1:5). Pray and pray more.

Since ancient days, Christians have always sought to persevere in their faith, in their prayers, and in their efforts to live out their faith by putting their faith into action. Prayer is action. Sometimes it has the appearance of being by form or pattern. But this is not the end in itself. Rather, prayer is always action in that it is the human being speaking to God or listening to God. That is prayer. In prayer, we pray, "Now to him who is able to accomplish far more than all we ask or imagine, by the power at work within us" (Eph 3:20). We pray tirelessly because our Lord always hears the cries of our heart.

Prayer is that spiritual conversation one has with our Lord. There have been many saints who came from simple backgrounds, but because they chose to believe and grow in prayer, they lived lives in which they, with God's great guidance, were able to move mountains. We can do this today. Pray and pray more. Pray saying words, but learn to pray in silence and by listening. Pray and persevere in your prayer. Prayer is one of the greatest powers we possess as human beings. Use this great gift from God and come closer to the Lord. In humility, give thanks to the Lord our God.